HANDS OFF!

SELF-DEFENSE for WOMEN

By MAJOR W. E. FAIRBAIRN

Author of
GET TOUGH!

Photographs by
MAJOR F. A. R. LEITAO
Shanghai Volunteer Corps

The Naval & Military Press Ltd

Published by

The Naval & Military Press Ltd
Unit 5 Riverside, Brambleside
Bellbrook Industrial Estate
Uckfield, East Sussex
TN22 1QQ England

Tel: +44 (0) 1825 749494

www.naval-military-press.com
www.nmarchive.com

This book is published strictly for historical purposes.
The Naval & Military Press Ltd expressly bears no responsibility or liability of any type,
to any first, second or third party, for any harm, injury, or loss whatsoever.

In reprinting in facsimile from the original, any imperfections are inevitably reproduced
and the quality may fall short of modern type and cartographic standards.

NOTE

There are many persons with an erroneous impression concerning the Art of Jiu-jitsu. Quite a number of them are under the impression that it is only necessary to take one or two lessons, after which they will be able to throw their opponents over their heads. There are others who believe that immediately a Jiu-jitsu expert catches hold of his opponent he will, by some secret Oriental method, throw him and break his arm or leg or render him unconscious. The reason for this being so generally believed is partly the fact that any two persons, without the slightest knowledge of any method of wrestling, could, with a few rehearsals, stage a demonstration that would easily deceive those not acquainted with the art, and partly the present day public demand for the spectacular.

THE AUTHOR

FOREWORD

It goes without saying that a woman should always know how to protect herself. In war time—in America at war—this is doubly so. Whether you carry on at home or in business, or whether you free a man for the front by taking his place on the assembly line or on the farm, the confidence you will gain from having learned to protect yourself, from knowing that you are the master of any unpleasant situation with which you may have to deal, will immeasurably increase your efficiency and value to the war effort. I hope that this book will be widely read, and I know that the result will be as I have said.

The basic methods of attack and defense in hand-to-hand fighting—described in my previous book, "Get Tough!"— were carefully worked out and developed during my many years service with the Shanghai Municipal Police. Those methods were designed primarily for use by men, though it is true that many of them are quite feasible for women. The methods of self-defense explained and illustrated in the present volume, however, have been especially selected for use by women, taking into account the usual disadvantages of weight, build, and strength. They are all practicable, and many are original, worked out in answer to the question: *What should I do were I to be attacked like this?*

It is to be expected that some of the more drastic measures advocated here will perhaps be considered distasteful and shocking. It is quite natural to feel this way, but a moment's consideration will, I am sure, convince the reader that any methods—so long as they be effective—are justifiable against a ruthless assailant.

In conclusion, a word about the handbag, handkerchief, or

glove which are frequently mentioned as effective weapons of defense. In the hands of an expert, yes; but the average woman, as compared to a man, is handicapped far too much in weight and strength to rely upon disposing of her assailant by a flick in the eye with one of these articles. Such a measure would doubtless only enrage him. The twenty methods to follow are enough. Study them carefully, practice them diligently, and, if the time ever comes when you must use them, put them into effect suddenly and without restraint. To take the battle into your opponent's camp, to catch him off his guard, is seventy-five per cent of the battle won.

W. E. FAIRBAIRN

CONTENTS

		PAGE
1	Wrist Hold (One Hand)	2
2	Wrist Hold (Two Hands)	3
3	Being Strangled (One Hand)	5
4	How to Apply the "Chin Jab"	7
5	Being Strangled (Two Hands)	9
6	"Bear Hug"—From in Front	10
7	"Bear Hug"—From Behind	11
8	Waist Hold—From in Front	13
9	Waist Hold—From Behind	15
10	Hair Hold—From Behind	17
11	Coat Hold	19
12	Coat Hold	21
13	Belt Hold	23
14	Simple Counters	25
15	Umbrella Drill	27
16	Being Held from in Front	29
17	The Theatre Hold	33
18	Matchbox (Warning)	37
19	Car "Hold-Up"	39
20	"Give Me a Light"	41

DEFENSE AGAINST VARIOUS HOLDS

No. 1. Wrist Hold (One Hand)

Your assailant seizes your right wrist with his left hand, Fig. 1. To make him release his hold: bend your arm from the elbow, upwards and towards your body, then twist your wrist towards and over his thumb, Fig. 2.

Note: The above must be one continuous movement and carried out with speed.

Fig. 1

Fig. 2

DEFENSE AGAINST VARIOUS HOLDS

No. 2. Wrist Hold (Two Hands)

Your assailant seizes you by both wrists, Fig. 3. To make him release his hold: bend your arms towards your body and twist your wrists in the direction of his thumbs.

Or: jerk your hands towards your body, at the same time hitting him in the face with the top of your head, Fig. 4.

Fig. 3

Fig. 4

Fig. 5

Fig. 6

DEFENSE AGAINST VARIOUS HOLDS

No. 3. Being Strangled (One Hand)

Your assailant seizes you by the throat with his right hand, forcing you back against a wall, Fig. 5.

1. With a sharp blow of your right hand strike his right wrist towards your left-hand side.//
2. If necessary, knee him in the pit of the stomach with your right knee, Fig. 6.

Note: The position demonstrated in Fig. 5 (Forced back against a wall) was selected because it shows the only position where it would be possible, by means of a Strangle Hold, for an assailant to do you any harm. In the event of anyone attempting to strangle you with only one hand, and you are clear of a wall or other obstruction, all that is necessary to break the hold, is suddenly to step backwards or sideways in the direction of his thumb.

The best demonstration of defense against this One-Hand Hold is the position shown in Fig. 5—Against a Wall. Further, if your assailant puts all his strength and weight into the hold, so much the better. A sharp blow as in Fig. 6, with the palm of the right hand on the thumbside of his wrist, is all that is necessary to make him release his hold.

Fig. 7

Fig. 8

Fig. 9

DEFENSE AGAINST VARIOUS HOLDS

No. 4. How to Apply the "Chin Jab"

In Defense Holds No. 5, Being Strangled (Two Hands); No. 8, Waist Hold From the Front; and No. 10, Hair Hold (From Behind), it will be noted one of the methods is referred to as a "Chin Jab." This blow is struck with the base or heel of the palm of the hand at the "Point of the Chin," and, if applied correctly, is liable to render your assailant unconscious.

CAUTION: The "Chin Jab" should be used only when circumstances justify such drastic methods. Students are advised to practice at "Shadow Drill," not on their friends.

1. Bend the right arm from the elbow, turning the palm of the hand to the front, Fig. 7.
2. Bend the palm of the hand backwards as far as possible, extending the fingers and thumb, and keep them bent (Fig. 8) so that, in the event of your missing your assailant's chin, they will reach his eyes, should the situation justify such drastic action.

Note: The force of this blow does not depend upon the strength of the person applying it, but upon keeping the palm of the hand bent backwards. This permits one to deliver a "rock-crushing" blow with a follow-through from the shoulder and no possibility of hurting one's own hand when applying it.

3. The position of the hand in Fig. 8 was selected as the best to demonstrate the relative position of the fingers, thumb, and palm of the hand. Students will find that a position somewhat as in Fig. 9 will be a more practical position from which to start this blow.

Fig. 10

DEFENSE AGAINST VARIOUS HOLDS

No. 5. Being Strangled (Two Hands)

Your assailant seizes you by the throat with both hands, forcing you back against a wall, Fig. 10.

Note: In the event of being attacked in this manner, drastic methods are called for and are justifiable. We strongly recommend the application of the "Chin Jab."

1. Turn up the whites of your eyes to deceive your assailant and put him off his guard. Then suddenly shoot both your hands up inside his arms and strike him on the point of the chin—"Chin Jab."

2. Keep your fingers and thumbs extended and endeavour to reach his eyes with the points of your fingers or thumb of one of your hands. Simultaneously knee him in the pit of the stomach, Fig. 10.

DEFENSE AGAINST VARIOUS HOLDS

No. 6. "Bear Hug" (From in Front)

Your assailant, with both arms, seizes you around the body, imprisoning your arms, Fig. 11.

1. Kick him on the shins.
2. Knee him in the pit of the stomach.
3. Stamp on his feet.
4. Bump him in the face with your head.

Fig. 11

DEFENSE AGAINST VARIOUS HOLDS

No. 7. "Bear Hug" (From Behind)

Your assailant, with both arms, seizes you around the body, imprisoning your arms, Fig. 12.

1. Stamp on his feet.
2. Kick him on the shins.
3. Bump him in the face with the back of your head.

Fig. 12

Fig. 13

Fig. 14

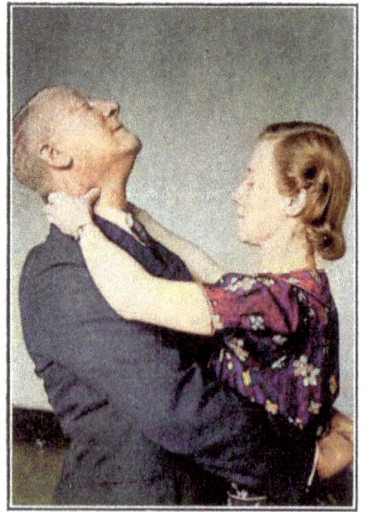

DEFENSE AGAINST VARIOUS HOLDS

No. 8. Waist Hold (From in Front)

Your assailant seizes you around the body from in front, leaving your arms free.

1. Place your left hand around and in to the small of his back, simultaneously striking him on the point of the chin ("Chin Jab"). If necessary, knee him in the stomach, Fig. 13.

2. Seize his neck with both hands, fingers touching behind, thumbs in front, the points one on either side of the "Adam's apple." Force inwards and upwards with the points of your thumbs and towards you with the points of your fingers—then jerk his head sharply backwards, Fig. 14.

Note: The average person is very susceptible to the discomfort caused by this neck hold as shown in Fig. 14, and students are advised not to practice it on their friends.

Fig. 15

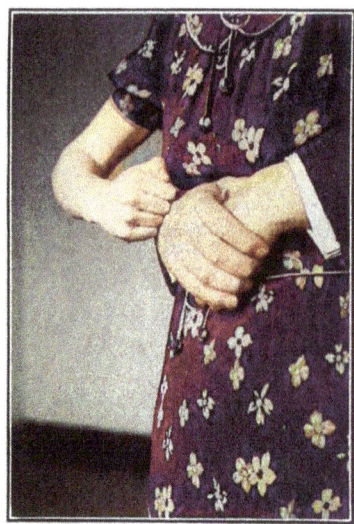

Fig. 15A

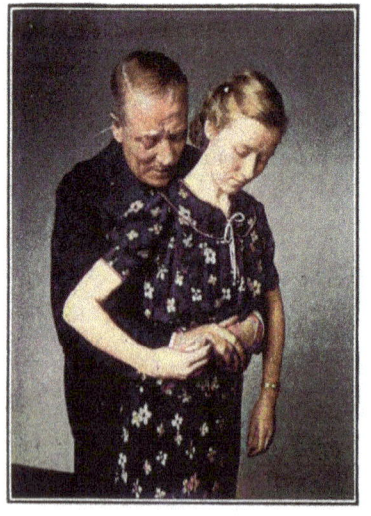

Fig. 16

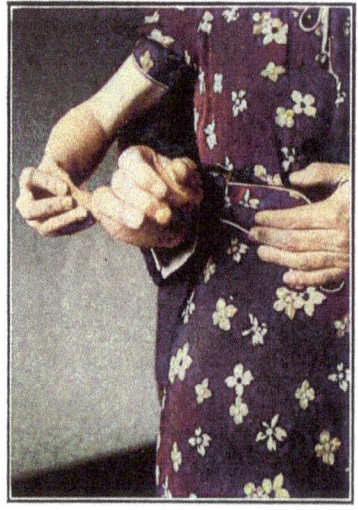

Fig. 16A

DEFENSE AGAINST VARIOUS HOLDS

No. 9. Waist Hold (From Behind)

Your assailant seizes you around the waist from behind, leaving your arms free.

1. Strike the back of his hand a sharp blow with your knuckles, Figs. 15 and 15A.
2. Seize either of his little fingers and bend it backwards; if necessary, break it, Figs. 16 and 16A.

Note: It should be noted that the little-finger hold is the only hold on the fingers that is effective. There are many persons who could stand the pain of having one of their other fingers broken, but it is fairly safe to state that not more than one person in a hundred could stand the pain of having the little finger treated in the same way. Further, it is a sure method of making your assailant release his hold.

3. Stamp on his feet with the heel of your shoe simultaneously striking him in the face with the back of your head.

Fig. 17

Fig. 18

Fig. 19

DEFENSE AGAINST VARIOUS HOLDS

No. 10. Hair Hold (From Behind)

Your assailant seizes you by the hair, from behind, with his right hand.

1. Bend backwards and seize his hand from above, keeping a firm grip with your hands, force your head into his hand to prevent him letting go, Fig. 17.
2. Turn in towards your assailant; this will twist his wrist.
3. Force your head up and bend his wrist inwards, away from his elbow, Fig. 18.

Note: The success of this method depends mainly upon the speed with which it is completed and the continuous upward pressure of your head against his hand, combined with the firm grip on his hand by both of yours.

If, when you are in the position shown in Fig. 18, your assailant attempts to use his left hand against you, immediately release your hold with the right hand and strike him on the point of the chin ("Chin Jab"), Fig. 19.

Fig. 20

Fig. 21

Fig. 22

DEFENSE AGAINST VARIOUS HOLDS

No. 11. Coat Hold

Your assailant seizes you by the left shoulder with his right hand, Fig. 20.

1. Seize his right hand with your right hand and prevent him from releasing his hold.

2. Seize his right elbow with your left hand, your thumb to the left, Fig. 21.

3. With a circular upward and then downward motion of your left hand on the elbow, turn sharply outwards towards your right-hand side by pivoting on your right foot and stepping across his front with your left leg, Fig. 22.

4. Keep a firm grip with your right hand to prevent him releasing his hold and apply a downward pressure on his elbow with your left hand.

Note: It should be noted in Nos. 11 and 12, Coat Holds, and No. 13, Belt Hold, that your assailant having caught hold of your clothing, etc., has placed himself at a great disadvantage and it is for this reason that you should endeavour to prevent him from releasing his hold until you have effectively dealt with him.

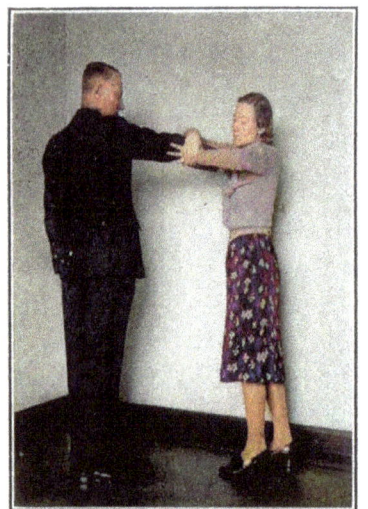

Fig. 23

Fig. 24

DEFENSE AGAINST VARIOUS HOLDS

No. 12. Coat Hold

Your assailant seizes you by the left shoulder with his right hand.

1. Seize his right elbow with your left hand from underneath; at the same time pass your right hand over the arm and seize the elbow with your right hand above your left, Fig. 23.

2. With a circular upward and downward motion of your hands on his elbow turn sharply outwards towards your right-hand side. This will bring you into the position shown in Fig. 24.

3. Force his elbow towards your body and push up with your left shoulder. This will prevent him from releasing his arm. If necessary, smash him in the face with your right knee.

Fig. 25

Fig. 26

DEFENSE AGAINST VARIOUS HOLDS

No. 13. Belt Hold

Your assailant seizes you by the belt with his right hand.

1. Seize his right hand from above with your right hand and prevent him from releasing his hold.
2. Seize his right elbow with your left hand from underneath, thumb to the left, Fig. 25.

Note: The success of the method depends upon the correct position of your left hand upon your assailant's right elbow, and special attention must be paid to the position of your left thumb.

3. With a circular upward and then downward motion of your left hand on the elbow, turn sharply towards your right-hand side by pivoting on your right foot, simultaneously stepping across his front with your left leg. Fig. 26.

Note: Providing you have prevented him from releasing his hold of your belt this will be found to be a very effective hold.

Fig. 27

Fig. 27A

Fig. 28

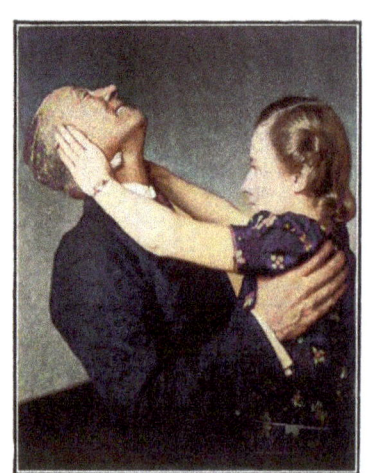

Fig. 28A

DEFENSE AGAINST VARIOUS HOLDS

No. 14. Simple Counters

(A) *Hand Shake:* It frequently happens that you meet a person who is very proud of his gripping powers and takes great pleasure, when shaking hands, in gripping your hand with all his strength, apparently with the idea of convincing you that he is a real "he-man," Fig. 27.

It is a very simple matter for you to take the conceit out of him—Place the *point* of your right thumb on the back of his hand between the thumb and index finger as in Fig. 27A.

Note: Only a very small amount of pressure with the point of your thumb is necessary to counteract his grip, and as the intention is to take the conceit out of him, do not make it obvious by applying more pressure than is necessary.

(B) *Against Being Lifted.* A person attempts to lift you up by catching hold of you under the arm-pits. To prevent this: force the points of your thumbs up and into his neck close alongside the jaw bone as in Figs. 28 and 28A. Push upwards and force his head slightly backwards, which will place him off balance, making it impossible for him to lift you.

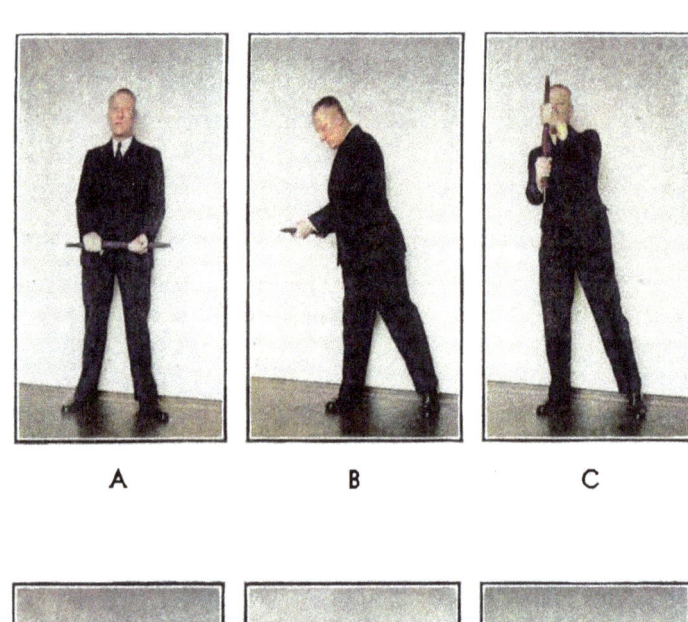
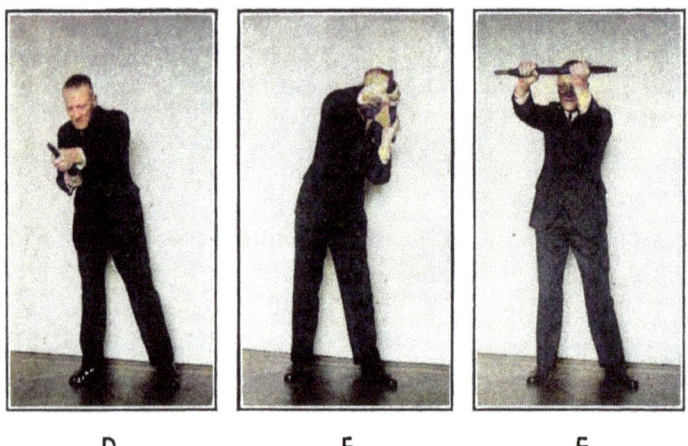

THE UMBRELLA AS A MEANS OF DEFENSE

No. 15. Umbrella Drill

The present-day umbrella, which is around 18 to 20 inches in length, is an ideal weapon for the purpose of defense against the more serious methods of attack, and students are advised to study and make themselves thoroughly acquainted with the application of the various blows, as demonstrated:

DRILL MOVEMENTS

A = Right hand above—left hand below.
   Point of umbrella to the left-hand side.
B = Point, across the stomach.
C = Point up under the chin.
D = Point, down the face.
E = Handle, up across the face.
F = Up under the chin—aim to strike your opponent's Adam's apple with the center of the umbrella.

   Note: In the following pages only one position of attack by an assailant has been shown. This is done so as not to confuse the student when learning. There are, of course, numerous other positions your assailant could adopt when attacking you, but, providing you make yourself proficient in the use of the umbrella, at least one or two of the "Drill Strokes," perhaps with a slight variation, will more than enable you to deal effectively with any assailant.

Fig. 29

Fig. 30

Fig. 31

Fig. 32

THE UMBRELLA AS A MEANS OF DEFENSE

No. 16. Being Held from in Front

CAUTION: Never attempt to strike your assailant over the head with your umbrella. The utmost injury that you could inflict with the handle of an umbrella would not be sufficient to make him release his hold, and would most likely only make him annoyed or angry with you. Further, a blow at the head, with any weapon such as a stick or umbrella, is in nine out of ten cases "telegraphed" that it is going to be given, with the result that it is a very simple matter to prevent its reaching its mark—see Fig. 29.

Having been "Held Up" as in Fig. 30, your assailant having hold of your shoulder or arms with one or both hands:

1. Hold your umbrella as in Fig. 31, right hand above, left hand below, with an interval of approximately six inches between your hands.

2. Strike your assailant with the point of the umbrella across the stomach, just below or above the belt line, by shooting your left hand forward and towards your right-hand side, simultaneously pulling the umbrella backwards with your right hand. This will bring your assailant to the position shown in Fig. 32.

[continued on page 31

Fig. 33

Fig. 34

Fig. 35

Fig. 36

THE UMBRELLA AS A MEANS OF DEFENSE

No. 16. Being Held from in Front (concl.)

3. Should your assailant still retain his hold (which is most unlikely), strike him under the chin with the point of the umbrella by jabbing upwards with both hands as in Fig. 33.

4. In the event of missing your assailant's chin with the point of the umbrella, strike at his face by hitting downwards with your left hand, simultaneously drawing back with your right hand as in Fig. 34.

5. Continue your defense by shooting your right hand forward and towards your left-hand side, striking your assailant across the face in the region of the nose with the handle of the umbrella as in Fig. 35.

6. If necessary, strike him under the chin as in Fig. 36.

Fig. 37

Fig. 38

Fig. 39

A DEFENSE AGAINST WANDERING HANDS

No. 17. The Theatre Hold

1. You are sitting on a chair and a hand is placed on your left knee as in Fig. 37.

2. Catch hold of the hand with your right hand, passing your fingers and thumb under the palm of the hand as in Fig. 38. Although it is rather essential that the initial hold of the offending hand should be as near as possible to that shown, you should not have any difficulty in obtaining it, as the person concerned will most likely be under the impression that you are simply returning his caress.

3. Keeping a firm grip on the hand, lift it from your knee, pulling it across your body towards your right-hand side, Fig. 39.

[continued on page 35

Fig. 40

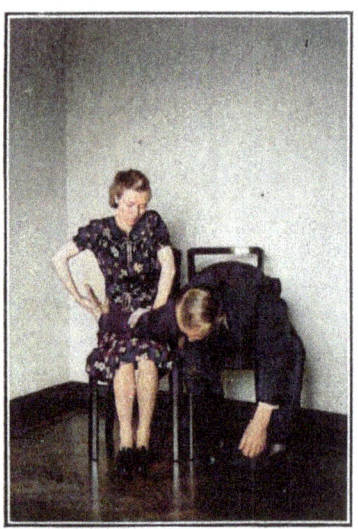
Fig. 41

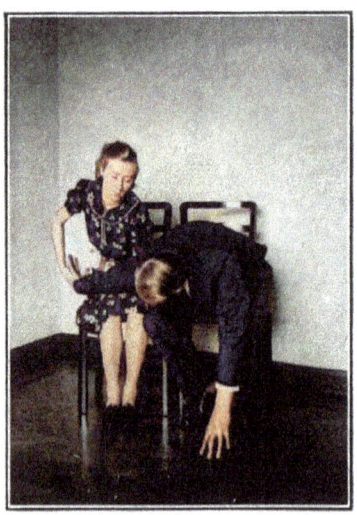
Fig. 42

A DEFENSE AGAINST WANDERING HANDS

No. 17. The Theatre Hold (concl.)

4. Twist the hand and arm away from you, simultaneously seizing his elbow from above, as in Fig. 40.
5. Force the arm downwards by pressing on the elbow with your left hand and twisting the arm with your right hand, until it is in the position shown in Fig. 41.
6. By your keeping a reasonable pressure on his elbow and a fairly firm grip of his hand, it is impossible for your opponent to move. An alternative method of holding your opponent is to apply pressure on his elbow with your left forearm as in Fig. 42.

Note: (A) For the purpose of clearness the various movements in The Theatre Hold have been demonstrated sitting in ordinary chairs in the front row. Had they been demonstrated as taking place in the second or back row, the opponent's head would have been smashed on to the backs of the front seats.

(B) Students should note that after their opponent's offending hand has been secured, as demonstrated in Fig. 38, all other movements of this hold are continuous. The amount of pain or discomfort inflicted on your opponent depends upon the speed with which the various movements are completed.

(C) If your opponent anticipates the application of this hold, it naturally follows that it might be difficult to apply. That being so—and the circumstances justifying it—we recommend the application of one of the Matchbox. Defenses as demonstrated on pages 37 to 41.

Fig. 43

THE MATCHBOX DEFENSE

No. 18. Matchbox (Warning)

The use of the matchbox is one of the most drastic methods of defense that it is possible to employ and must only be used when the situation calls for drastic action. Further, students are warned to be extremely careful when testing the force of the blow on themselves (Fig. 43), otherwise it is quite possible for them to render themselves unconscious.

The advantage of using a matchbox, as compared with a stick or other weapon, lies in the surprise and complete unexpectedness of this form of attack. Any person not previously aware of this method of defense, seeing you take an ordinary matchbox out of a purse or pocket, would not be suspicious or on his guard.

There are several situations in which the use of a matchbox might easily be the only possible means of defense:

(A) You are driving a car and have picked up a hitch-hiker; he suddenly sticks a gun in your ribs. (See page 39.)

(B) You are unexpectedly stopped on a dark road with a demand "Give me a light" or "Hand over the bag." (see page 41.)

Fig. 44, Fig. 45

Fig. 46

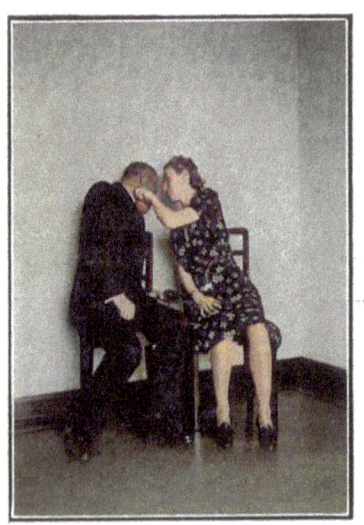

Fig. 47

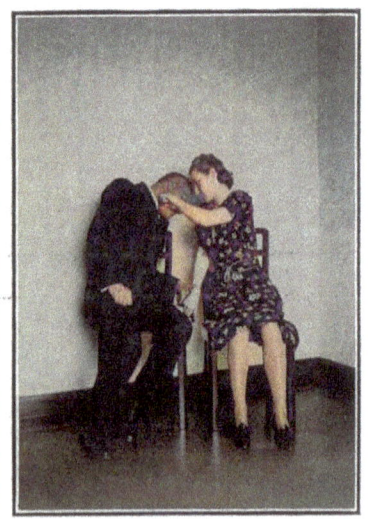

Fig. 48

THE MATCHBOX DEFENSE

No. 19. Car "Hold-Up"

You are driving a car (left-hand drive), and have picked up a hitch-hiker. He suddenly sticks a gun in your ribs.

1. Take the matchbox and hold it as in Fig. 44, the top of the box being slightly below the finger and thumb, the box resting, if possible, on the little finger, Fig. 45.

2. Keeping the upper part of the left arm firmly against the left side of your body, with a circular upward motion of your left hand, pivoting your body from the hip (Fig. 46), strike your opponent on the jaw bone, anywhere between the ear and the point of the chin, Fig. 47. Simultaneously, seize the gun from above with your right hand, turning the muzzle away from your body as in Fig. 48. If you have struck your opponent correctly he will be "OUT."

Note: (A) Students must in practice check up against the fatal error, committed by most, of "telegraphing" their intentions by drawing back their striking hand. The blow starts from the original position of the hand when the matchbox was first put into position. The strength or force of the blow depends mainly upon the follow-through of the body, not in the strength of the arm.

(B) In the event of your opponent being on your left-hand side, take the matchbox in your right hand; the blow will be equally effective.

Fig. 49

Fig. 50

Fig. 51

THE MATCHBOX DEFENSE

No. 20. "Give Me a Light"

You are unexpectedly stopped on a dark road with a demand, "Give me a light" or "Hand over your bag."

The usual method of approach is for your assailant suddenly to step out of an alleyway or from behind a tree as you are about to pass, when your position would be somewhat as shown in Fig. 49.

1. Take the matchbox as in Fig. 50, the top of the box being slightly below the finger and thumb, the box resting, if possible, on the little finger.

2. It should be noted that the method of striking is somewhat different from that shown previously. In Fig. 51, your opponent being on his feet and very close to you, the blow must be delivered upwards. The force of the blow depends on the follow-through, which in this case is from the right hip, leg, and foot.

Note: An alternative method—if the situation is serious enough to justify such drastic action—is: take a matchbox with the heads of the matches on top—strike a match and set fire to the matches, immediately throwing it into your assailant's face.

(1)

www.ingramcontent.com/pod-product-compliance
Lightning Source LLC
Chambersburg PA
CBHW061250230426
43663CB00022B/2969